ROUND AND ROUND THE GARDEN

First presented by the Library Theatre Co., Scarborough in June 1973 and subsequently by the Greenwich Theatre Company in May 1974, and in London by Michael Codron at the Globe Theatre in August 1974, with the following cast of characters:

Norman	Tom Courtenay
Tom	Michael Gambon
Sarah	Penelope Keith
Annie	Felicity Kendal
Reg	Mark Kingston
Ruth	Bridget Turner

The play directed by Eric Thompson
Setting by Alan Pickford

The action passes in the garden of a Victorian vicarage-type house during a week-end in July

ACT I
    Scene 1   Saturday, 5.30 p.m.
    Scene 2   Saturday, 9 p.m.

ACT II
    Scene 1   Sunday, 11 a.m.
    Scene 2   Monday, 9 a.m.

Period – the present

ACT ONE

Scene 1

The garden. Saturday, 5.30 p.m.

The garden is overlooked by a Victorian, country-vicarage-type house with terrace and french windows leading directly into the sitting-room. Once obviously well laid out, it is now wildly overgrown. There is an entrance to the tennis-court and the road, and another—above an old statue and through some brambles—which leads round to the same direction: these also go to the front of the house

Tom, a thoughtful, pensive man, enters above the statue. He is casually dressed in week-end country clothes. He stands gazing rather aimlessly about him, then wanders down to the barrel, on which is a cup and saucer. He picks up the cup, and is surprised to find the saucer stuck to it. After considering this for a moment, he replaces cup and saucer

Annie enters from the tennis-court. Red-faced and shiny, she wears a very old sweater, button-up and too large, jeans and gumboots. She also has on a pair of gardening gloves and carries six roses and a pair of scissors. She stops on seeing Tom

Annie (*casually*) Oh, Tom. Hallo.
Tom Hallo, Annie.
Annie Didn't know you were here this afternoon.
Tom Yes. I thought I'd just look up your cat if I could. See that paw of his.
Annie Oh, yes, fine.
Tom I put a dressing on it but it's probably come off by now.
Annie Probably.

A pause

Tom Lovely day.
Annie Yes.
Tom You'll be going off soon, I take it.
Annie Yes.
Tom Oh. Have a good time.
Annie Thanks.
Tom Don't get lost.
Annie I can't get far in a day. Any sign of Reg and Sarah?
Tom Haven't seen them.
Annie Hope they're not going to be late. I'll have to hang on till they come just to make sure they know where everything is for Mother.

Tom Yes.

Annie She's been lying up there moaning all day because I'm going away. You'd think I was off for a year, instead of a couple of nights.

Tom I'll look in if you like. Make sure they're coping.

Annie They'll manage.

Tom Nice of them to offer, wasn't it?

Annie Sarah and Reg?

Tom Yes.

Annie (*putting five roses on the terrace and clipping the sixth*) Why shouldn't they? She's his mother, too, after all. It's high time they did offer. They get off very lightly. So does Ruth for that matter. They're all perfectly happy to leave me to cope for nine-tenths of the year. The least they can do is to spare me a couple of days. Not that I'll ever get Ruth to do anything. Far too busy with her high finance. But Reg and Sarah are perfectly capable . . .

Tom Quite.

Annie What will you be doing?

Tom When?

Annie This week-end.

Tom Oh, you know. Mooching about.

Annie On your own?

Tom Probably.

Annie That's what I'll be doing.

Tom Ah. Well, I'll think of you, wherever you are, mooching about while I'm—mooching about here.

Annie Thanks. (*Pause*) Silly, really.

Tom What?

Annie Well—both of us in different parts of the country, stuck on our own . . .

Tom Yes. Funny thing, life.

Annie Yes. (*Pause*) What's the time?

Tom Er—just gone five-thirty.

Annie Oh.

Tom When are you leaving?

Annie I'm catching the bus in the village. That's providing Reg and Sarah arrive in time.

Tom I can run you down in the car.

Annie No . . .

Tom If you look like being . . .

Annie No, I'd rather walk.

Tom Won't you have a case?

Annie No. It's all right. I don't mind carrying suitcases. I quite enjoy it. The walk . . .

Tom Oh. Any idea where that cat is?

Annie Probably outside here somewhere. I must get on. Prepare for my lone trip.

Tom See you before you go then.

Annie Yes.

Tom Better search out my patient. (*Calling*) Pussy, puss, puss . . .

Tom goes off by the tennis-court

Annie stands for a moment looking after Tom

Annie (*at length, exasperated*) Oh . . .

Annie goes off to the house, taking the cup and saucer

A pause

Norman enters stealthily by the statue. Despite the bright sunshine of the late July afternoon, he has on a rather grimy mac and a woolly hat. He is bearded, a rather aimless sort of beard. He carries a battered cardboard suitcase. Not surprisingly, he is perspiring furiously. As the house comes into his view, he stops, smiles to himself, puts down his case and, at peace with the world, breathes in the country air

Tom (*off, distant*) Kitty—kitty—kitty—cat—cat—cat—kitty—kitty—kitty . . .

Norman, on hearing this, dives swiftly for cover, forgetting his case which he leaves standing in the middle of the path. Tom's voice fades into the distance. Norman remains hidden

Annie enters and picks up the remaining roses. She stops as she sees Norman's case. She approaches, curious, and stares at it. She looks about her

Annie Hallo? Anyone about?
Norman (*hidden, muffled*) Annie . . .

Annie stares about her

Annie . . .
Annie Norman?
Norman (*showing himself*) Annie!
Annie Oh—you've come . . .
Norman Yes.
Annie But what are you . . . ?
Norman I couldn't wait. I had to see you.
Annie But we agreed . . . Oh, Norman, honestly. You are the limit . . .
Norman (*passionately*) Oh, my darling . . . (*He moves romantically to her but stops suddenly. With a cry*) Oh—God!
Annie (*alarmed*) What's the matter?
Norman These bloody brambles. Why doesn't somebody clear these bloody brambles?
Annie Hang on—stop flailing about . . . (*She takes his hand to pull him clear*)

Norman (*yelling*) Don't pull! Don't pull! It's impaled in my leg.

Annie (*bending to free him*) All right. Wait—wait . . .

Norman Aaaah!

Annie Ssh.

Norman You must have hands like asbestos. (*As Annie frees him*) Aaah! Aaah! Aaah! (*Hopping away and sitting on the barrel*) God!

Annie Mother's resting, you know. You'll wake her up.

Norman (*rolling up his trouser leg*) Look at this. I'm scratched right down my leg.

Annie If Mother's woken up before she's ready to wake up, she doesn't know where she is. It takes me an hour to explain.

Norman Look, blood—bleeding . . .

Annie Let's see. (*She bends to look*)

Norman Careful! Deformed for life.

Annie Hold these. (*She hands Norman the roses*)

Norman (*taking them and dropping them immediately with another yell*) Aaah!

Annie Ssh.

Norman It's a death trap, this garden.

Annie Look, will you please be quiet.

Norman Only been here two minutes, lost three pints of blood. (*He sucks his hand*)

Annie Oh, Norman, do shut up. You're so weedy.

Norman (*indignantly*) Weedy? (*He rises*)

Annie A real weed. (*She starts to pick up the flowers*)

Norman (*romantic again*) Oh, Annie . . . (*He reaches out and touches her leg*)

Annie (*pulling away, irritated*) Don't. Just a minute.

Norman stares at her a second, then sits again

Norman I'm exhausted.

Annie I should think so. In that coat.

Norman It was raining in Fulham.

Annie Was it?

Norman Metaphorically it was.

Annie Oh.

Norman (*expansively*) Ah, the sun, the sun, the sun . . .

Annie Norman . . .

Norman Mmm?

Annie What are you doing here?

Norman laughs secretively

No, seriously, Norman. What's the point of our making all these arrangements, of trying to make absolutely sure no-one was going to get upset—no-one was going to get hurt and then you turn up here.

Norman I wanted to see you. I was frightened you'd changed your mind.

Annie But I'm supposed to meet you. We're supposed to meet. In the village, at the back of the post office, seven o'clock.

Norman I got here early.

Annie Well, you'll have to go away for an hour. I haven't even packed.

Norman Where am I supposed to go?

Annie I don't know. Go and walk round the Abbey.

Norman That's five miles away. I'm not walking five miles, just to wander round some ruin with a suitcase.

Annie I don't want you here when Reg and Sarah arrive. And I've got to see them in. I've got to show them where everything is for Mother. All her bottles and pills and God knows what. And which is their towel. I mean, there's masses. I can't just rush off. Anyway, Tom's here . . .

Norman (*scornfully*) Tom.

Annie He's only round the front of the house, looking for the cat.

Norman Tom. Ha!

Annie And don't say it like that. I don't say Ruth, ha!

Norman I don't mind if you do. I say it.

Annie Not to her face, you don't.

Norman How do you know?

Annie I bet you don't. I've seen you with her.

Norman How do you know what I say to her face behind your back?

Annie I know you. More important I know my sister.

Norman She'll have got my note by now.

Annie Note?

Norman Telling all.

Annie All what?

Norman It's all over between us. That ever since we stayed here last Christmas, something wonderful happened. You and I were all that mattered. That everything else . . .

Annie You didn't? You didn't say that?

Norman That the love between us . . .

Annie If you said that, I warn you, I'll ring her up this minute . . . (*She moves away*)

Norman (*alarmed*) Where are you going?

Annie To ring her up.

Norman All right, all right. I didn't. I didn't leave her a note. Promise.

Annie Promise?

Norman Promise.

Annie So long as you haven't. I mean—well, after all she is my sister. I'm fond of her. Quite. We've already agreed it's stupid to—upset everything just for us. We're being terribly adult, aren't we? You said we were—in your letter . . . Far better we two just go away quietly to a little hotel somewhere, get it all off our chests—out of our system—God, I'm making it sound like a laxative—you know what I mean—work it all off, that's what I mean. Then you go back to Ruth and live happily ever after—or as happily as you can seeing it's Ruth and I come back to Mother and—and—look after her . . .

Norman And then? When your mother finally pegs out?

Annie Oh well. I'll face that when it comes.

Norman Yes, you'll have to.

Annie There's Tom. He's hovering in the background.

Norman The creeping vet.

Annie He's done a lot to help here, you know. He did all the kitchen ceiling for me. Two coats. He's a jolly good vet, too. He has a marvellous way with animals. Actually, he's better with them than he is with people really.

Norman You'll have to start going around on all fours then, won't you.

Annie Oh, shut up. I don't know why you're so nasty about him, he likes you very much.

Norman He takes you for granted. Here you are—a beautiful girl. Vibrant. He could marry you tomorrow. He could make you happy. And what does he do? He spends more time with that cat than he does with you.

Annie Well, he's a vet, isn't he?

Norman Vet. V.E.T. Very Egocentric Twit. He doesn't deserve you.

Annie And you do?

Norman No. But I'm strangely engaging.

Annie No, you're not, you're foul. I don't think I want to come with you after all. I've changed my mind. I'll give Mother a blanket bath, it'll be much more fun.

Norman I love you.

Annie Oh, Norman . . . When you look like that, I almost believe you. You look like a—what are those things?

Norman Greek gods. (*He does a "Greek god" attitude*)

Annie Old English sheepdogs.

Norman Oh, great.

Annie They're super dogs. All woolly and double-ended.

Norman I'm not woolly and double-ended.

Annie You are a bit. You're like a badly built haystack.

Norman I'm going.

Annie Yes, you'd better before Tom . . .

Norman (*taking her hand, suddenly very serious and intense*) Good-bye, my darling.

Annie (*suppressing her laughter*) Oh, Norman, do stop it.

Norman What?

Annie Oh, I'm sorry, I . . . (*She starts laughing*)

Norman (*hurt*) What?

Annie It's just you're so—terribly quaint.

Norman (*huffily*) If it's quaint to be romantic . . . I mean, if you prefer me to knock you down . . .

Annie Try it.

Norman If that's what you want. Where's the romance? Where's the romance gone? Destroyed by the cynics and liberationists. Woe betide the man who dares to pay a woman a compliment today—he bends to kiss her hand and wham—the old karate chop on the back of the neck and she's away with his wallet. Forget the flowers, the chocolates, the soft word—rather woo her with a self-defence manual in one hand and a family planning leaflet in the other.

Annie Oh, Norman, you are stupid.

Norman Yes. I really do love you, Annie.

Annie Do you?

Norman Yes.

Annie That's a pity.

Norman Why?

Annie For everyone. Golly, look at this garden. It's like a jungle. Old Mr Purdy's got his leg again. He's been off a fortnight.

Norman (*uninterested*) Oh.

Annie Mrs Purdy says it's a war wound but I think it's gout. He's a terrific drinker. All day. The potting shed's full of his empties. He says they're for weed killer but he's got enough there to defoliate the whole of Sussex. If you look out of the window at tea time, you can see him draped over his spade. Like an old bag of fertilizer . . .

Norman Seven o'clock, then, back of the post office. (*He goes to move*)

Annie Seven o'clock. I say, it's awfully exciting in a way, isn't it? I mean, do you know I haven't been away from this place for nearly two years, what with Mother and one thing and another. I'm longing to see the sea again. I've forgotten what it looks like.

Norman Ah.

Annie Where did you say we were going? Hastings. Why did you choose Hastings?

Norman Well—it looks sort of close on the map.

Annie I'm not complaining. I mean, I'm sure Hastings is super.

Norman Yes. As a matter of fact, I wasn't able to get a vacancy after all —not in Hastings.

Annie Oh.

Norman It's summer, you see.

Annie Yes, I've noticed.

Norman Ah, well, I'd forgotten.

Annie So we're not going to Hastings?

Norman I'm afraid not.

Annie Where are we going?

Norman Well, I managed after a bit of trouble to get us fixed up in East Grinstead. They had a cancellation.

Annie (*digesting this*) Oh, well. Super. East Grinstead, then. I haven't been there, either.

Norman It was the best I could do. It's on the way to Hastings.

Annie Lovely.

Norman (*leering*) Not that we'll see much of it—eh?

Annie (*blankly*) How do you mean?

Norman Well . . .

Annie Oh. (*Doubtfully*) Oh, yes. (*She thinks*) I expect we'll want some fresh air at some stage though, won't we? I mean, we won't—all the time. I mean, if it's a hotel they'll want to make the beds and—change the soap—so I expect we'll get time for a bit of a snoop around, just a bit.

Norman (*unconvinced*) Oh, yes . . .

Annie It'd be a shame to go all the way to East Grinstead and then not see anything of it at all. I mean, what the hell, let's do what we said and have a really *dirty* week-end. I mean, absolutely *filthy* but, you know, if it's all . . . Makes Jill a dull girl. (*She laughs*) God, I'm putting this awfully badly.

Norman You've just pulled a button off.

Annie Mmm?

Norman Your woolly thing. You've just pulled the button off.

Annie (*finding it in her hand, absently*) Oh, yes. (*She puts the button in her pocket*)

They are both embarrassed now

Norman I stopped off in the village. Bought some new pyjamas.

Annie Oh. Super. In my honour?

Norman Yes.

Annie Better than wearing the same ones you do with Ruth.

Norman Yes.

Annie I mean, just because you're unfaithful there's no need for your pyjamas to be as well.

Norman No.

Annie I'm afraid you'll have to put up with my sensible flannelette. They're quite pretty but they're going round the knees and elbows.

Norman Ah.

A pause

Annie Well.

Norman Yes.

A pause

Would you like to have a look at my pyjamas now?

Annie Well, I . . .

Norman A sort of sneak preview.

Annie I think I'd rather wait until . . . (*She pauses—listens*) Was that the bell?

Norman Bell?

Annie Ssh. Mother's bell. She's awake. Now, you must go. See you at seven. (*As she hurries into the house*) I'll have a bath before I leave.

Annie goes into the house

Norman stares after her. He stands looking uncertain. He opens his case and removes a pair of cellophane-wrapped pyjamas. He stares at them critically. He places them on the statue and steps back to see what effect they have from a distance

Tom (*off*) Kitty—kitty—kitty . . .

Norman hides behind the statue

Tom enters from the tennis-court

Cat—cat—cat—kitty—kitty—kitty. (*He spies the cat up a tall tree*) Ah, there you are.

Norman appears, staring in disbelief. Tom turns from looking up at the tree, sees the case, stares at it, turns, and sees Norman

Oh, hallo, Norman. Didn't know you were here.

Norman Tom. (*He shakes Tom's hand*)

Tom You and Ruth down to lend a hand, are you?

Norman How do you mean?

Tom With Annie going away. Are you down to help out?

Norman More or less.

Tom Where's Ruth?

Norman She's not here.

Tom Oh. I thought you said she was.

Norman No, I never said she was. You're the one who said she was.

Tom (*deciding he has lost the thread of this conversation*) Look at that daft animal.

Norman Mmm?

Tom See it? The cat—up there.

Norman Oh, yes.

Tom (*calling*) Avoiding me—aren't you? (*To Norman*) Septic paw.

Norman Uggh.

Tom Last time I looked at it, we two had a mild disagreement. (*To the cat*) Didn't we? Yes. (*To Norman*) Not the most sociable animal.

Norman Vicious brute. Kills on sight for pleasure.

Tom Well, I can't really treat a patient who's thirty foot up a tree. Think I'll call it a day. No way of luring him down.

Norman You could sling a brick at it.

Tom Hardly.

Norman Breach of professional etiquette?

Tom Something of the sort. (*Seeing Norman's pyjamas*) Good Lord, what on earth are those?

Norman Ssh. They look like wild pyjamas. Don't disturb them, they're nesting.

Tom Yours, are they?

Norman Yes. I better put them away before they savage someone. (*Snatching them, pretending they are attacking him, then cramming them back in the suitcase*) Go on, get in you brutes. In, in—get in. (*He slams the lid triumphantly*) The tops are all right, it's the bottoms you've got to watch.

Tom (*impassive through this*) Seen Annie yet?

Norman No. Yes. Why?

Tom Well. What's your opinion?

Norman What of?

Tom Man to man? Between you and me?

Norman What?

Tom I mean, it's very odd, isn't it?

Norman What is?

Tom Her holiday. I mean, there's nothing wrong in having a holiday, but why the mystery?

Norman Mystery?

Tom Practically sneaking off. Won't say where she's going. What she's going to do.

Norman Perhaps she doesn't want people to know.

Tom Not like Annie, that. She's usually very open. Frank sort of person. No secrets. Know what I mean?

Norman Really.

Tom I mean, I've known her a long time . . .

Norman That doesn't give you ownership of her.

Tom No. Gives me interest. Concern.

Norman I should stick to coaxing cats out of trees.

Tom (*thoughtfully*) Hastings.

Norman Eh?

Tom I've got a feeling she's set her sights on Hastings.

Norman Oh?

Tom She keeps bringing it up. In passing. You know—"Do you think it'll be warm in Hastings at this time of year?"—that sort of thing. Sometimes she tries to confuse the scent. Makes it Deal or Brighton. But Hastings is the commonest. I'm betting even money on Hastings. (*Calling*) Pussy—pussy—puss. This question is—and I'd like your advice on this, Norman . . . (*He pauses, gazing up into the tree*) The point is, Norman, should I or should I not offer to go to Hastings, too? I've been turning it over in my mind, should I or shouldn't I?

Norman No.

Tom Why is she going, I ask myself. Is she going as a gesture a covert invitation aimed at me? Is she asking me to come with her, in fact?

Norman No.

Tom Is she saying, I'm going to Hastings. If you care about me at all, you must come to Hastings?

Norman No.

Tom Having first, of course, told me, in so many words, by a series of hints exactly where she was going.

Norman Hastings.

Tom Yes.

Norman No. You've got the wrong end of the stick. If you want my opinion, that is subtle woman's language for stuff you, I'm off.

Tom No. I don't see that. I think I'll have to have it out with her.

Norman I wouldn't bother.

Tom I'm giving that cat up for today. Coming in?

Norman No, I'm going.

Tom Oh. I thought you said you were staying.

Norman No, I'm just passing through on my way to East Grinstead.

Tom Really? Business?

Norman Yes. International Association of Assistant Librarians Annual Conference.

Tom Jolly good.

Norman Exciting. (*Looking up in the tree*) Don't jump! Think of your wife and kittens.
Tom Well, I'd better pop in.

Tom starts to move towards the house. Norman picks up his case

Reg appears round the side of the house. He wears his cap and sports jacket and carries two suitcases, and a bundle of magazines tied with string

Reg Oy—oy.
Tom Ah!
Norman Oh, no.
Reg Hallo, hallo. Who's this shifty-looking pair?
Tom Hallo there, Reg.
Reg Tom. (*He slaps him*) Norm. Surprised to see you. You're both looking good. Both looking good.
Tom Yes—yes.
Reg What a day, eh? What a day. Ought to be knocking a ball about, eh? Well, that little lot took us—(*he checks his watch*)—sixty-two minutes exactly. Door to door. Forty-nine, nearly fifty miles as the crow flies. Know the trick? There's a trick to it. Don't take the A two-six-four. Take the A two-seven-two and then branch off on to the B two-one-three-nine. It looks longer but it isn't.
Tom I usually take the A two-eight-one.
Norman Oh, my God.
Reg (*laughing*) How long does that take you?
Tom About an hour and a half.
Reg Door to door?
Tom Yes.
Reg Well, it would. You're going round the houses. If you want to go that way, you'd do better to go through East Grinstead.
Norman (*jumping guiltily*) What, what?
Reg East Grinstead.
Norman Oh.
Tom Is Sarah here?
Reg Yes, yes. I think she went straight up to see Mother. (*Striding about*) Well, look at this for a day. What about this sunshine? Just the ticket. (*Spotting something in the tree*) Hallo, hallo. Anyone here a bird-watcher?
Norman Uh?
Reg Bird-watcher, are you? Like watching birds? (*He laughs*) What do you make of that? Eh? You're a vet. What do you make of that?
Tom Yes.
Norman Good gracious, it's a cat.
Reg Cat. (*He laughs*) See it? Cat.
Tom Silly creature.
Reg Mother's cat, isn't it?
Tom Yes.

Reg Oh. Before I forget. Got another vet joke for you.

Tom Oh, yes.

Reg (*putting his arm round Tom's shoulders*) Question: what happens when a vet walks through a deep puddle? Answer: he gets vater in his vellingtons.

Tom Ha!

Reg Vater in his vellingtons! Heard that the other day. Tickled me.

Norman Ha!

Reg What brings you here today, Norman? I didn't expect to see you. Ruth with you?

Norman No.

Reg Thank goodness for that. No offence, but thank goodness for that.

Tom He's passing through.

Norman Just passing through.

Reg Really?

Tom Going to East Grinstead.

Reg Ah, now. From here? You'll be going from here?

Norman Well, since this is where I am, it seems a good place to start.

Reg Turn left out of here—not right—through the village, then take the right fork past the pub—brings you on to the A two-seven-two. Save you ten miles.

Norman No, I don't fancy that way.

Reg Why not?

Norman I haven't got a car.

Reg Ah, well. Catch the bus.

Norman I'll do that.

Tom wanders to the house

Reg Where are you going?

Tom Just in.

Reg Try and persuade that wife of mine to put the kettle on.

Tom Ah.

Reg Ah!

Tom goes into the house

Norman How is she?

Reg Who?

Norman That wife of yours.

Reg I don't know. She's all right. When I last looked at her. (*He laughs*) Well now, what's going on?

Norman Eh?

Reg She off with Tom? Our Annie? Going off for a sly one with Tom?

Norman Is she?

Reg Obvious. As soon as she wrote to Sarah—asked us to come and look after Mother for the week-end—I thought, hallo, what's up.

Norman And Sarah?

Reg Sarah?

Norman What did she think?

Reg No idea. Didn't ask her. No, she's off with Tom. You could tell he was a bit on edge. Looked guilty. He must have been desperate.

Norman What do you mean, desperate?

Reg I mean. Knowing him. Not exactly one for taking the plunge, is he? Been hanging around here for, what, three years? And I bet you they haven't got further than a fumble on the sofa. Well, I'm glad. Glad for Annie. She's a bright girl. Not a great beauty but her heart's in the right place. Easy temperament, good around the house . . .

Norman All mod. cons., sunny view facing due south.

Reg What?

Norman You talk as if she's a property up for sale.

Reg No. No. All I'm saying . . .

Norman Better check her over for wood-worm while you're at it.

Reg (*laughing*) Check her over for wood-worm, I like that. (*Producing a bag from his pocket*) Want a toffee?

Norman Not at the moment.

Reg (*having one, the last in the bag*) What takes you to East Grinstead, then?

Norman Oh—business.

Reg Business?

Norman In a way.

Reg Oh, yes?

Norman (*winking*) Yes.

Reg (*laughing, knowingly*) Something lined up?

Norman You might say that.

Reg Bit of stuff?

Norman Just a little bit . . .

Reg Lucky chap. Hasn't got a friend, has she?

Norman She's got a sister but she's married.

Reg Oh, well. I'm not fussy. You're on.

Norman Reckon you'd get past Sarah?

Reg Ah. Well. Not seriously, no. (*He sits on the barrel*) I was only joking. I would never . . . Don't believe in that, personally. Mind you, I've been tempted. When you've been married a few years—you can't help window shopping. You know, the old urge. But you keep it under control, don't you? You have to. Well, *you* may not have to. But I have to. Not that there isn't something to be said for it. I've often thought it might actually help a marriage sometimes. It gets a bit stale, between you, you know. I'm not thinking just for me. For her, too. Sarah. I'm not being selfish. Perhaps if she—went off for a few days with someone— she might—well, it might make her a bit more—you know, give her a fresh—get her going again, for God's sake. If you follow me.

Norman Ah.

Reg Mind you, it'd never work for us. Sarah would never dream of going off. Pity. If she did, I could. But we're not like you and Ruth, you see.

Norman What are we like?

Reg Well—easier . . .

Norman There's nothing very easy about Ruth.

Reg No, I didn't mean easy like that, I meant—well, let's face it—you've always had, what shall we say—an unconventional relationship. Ruth was always a nonconformist, you know. Even when we were kids. I envy those types, sometimes. Mother was another, you know. In a different way. That old lady up there's had a life, I can tell you.

Norman I know.

Reg Wouldn't think so now. But she led our father a dance. Poor man really wasn't up to it. Shut himself in up there—pretended it all wasn't happening. Of course it was. Under his own roof sometimes. Well, it was bound to have an effect. Not so much on me—I was the eldest. Don't know what it did to Annie. She was younger. Think she just let it drift over her. Like she does now, most of the time. But Ruth. Ruth was altogether different.

Norman I know, I live with her.

Reg She took it—oddly.

Norman She's a mess.

Reg Putting it bluntly. She's got Mother's looks, mind you. Attractive, wouldn't you say? Difficult for a brother but—striking?

Norman Oh, yes.

Reg Annie and I always said she had our share, as well. Certainly had mine. I don't think Sarah married me for my looks.

Norman I wonder why she did.

Reg I don't know. That's a good question. I must ask her that sometime. (*He gets up*) Well, get going. She'll be looking for me. (*He picks up his suitcase*) Have a good trip. Think of me . . .

Norman I will.

Reg (*moving to the house, feeling the weight of his suitcase*) What the hell's she put in this one? Must have packed the bloody china cabinet. (*Turning back to Norman*) And another thing. We've got children. You haven't. That makes a difference. Can't go gallivanting off—not with children. Responsibilities. Blast it.

Sarah comes out from the house—smartly dressed in her summer best

Sarah Reg—oh. (*She sees Norman*) Hallo, Norman. (*She shakes his hand*)

Norman Hallo, Sarah. How's Sarah?

Sarah Very well, Norman. Surprised to hear you were here.

Norman Yes. Well, I was passing.

Sarah That's nice.

Norman Yes. Thought I'd look in on the old home.

Sarah Naturally.

Norman (*uneasy at her manner*) Well, I must be off. (*He gathers himself together and picks up his case, preparing to leave*)

Sarah Are you taking those in, Reg?

Reg Oh, yes. Yes . . . (*He starts to move in*)

Sarah I've just been talking to Annie.

Norman (*freezing in his tracks, warily*) Have you?

Sarah Yes. Oh, Reg, rather good news. She's decided she doesn't want to go away, after all.

Reg She doesn't?

Norman Eh?

Sarah No. Isn't that nice?

Reg Well, we needn't have bothered to come then.

Sarah I think it's just as well we did.

Reg (*going in*) All this racing about and we didn't need to come at all.

Reg goes inside

Sarah (*following him*) It gets difficult for her, coping entirely on her own ... (*Turning back and smiling brilliantly at Norman*) 'Bye, 'bye, Norman. I expect you'll want to hurry along to East Grinstead.

Sarah goes inside

Norman stands speechless with fury. He puts down his suitcase and paces up and down in silence for a second

Norman (*exploding with a fierce yell and kicking his suitcase frenziedly*) Damned—stupid—interfering—rotten—bitch!

Reg comes out to fetch the magazines he left behind

Reg Are you dashing off immediately or can you stay for a bit?

Norman I'm staying. You bet your sweet life I'm staying.

Norman snatches up his suitcase and strides angrily into the house. Reg, a little bewildered, follows him

CURTAIN

SCENE 2

The same. Saturday, 9 p.m.

Sarah and Reg come out from the house. They are supporting Norman who is very drunk

Sarah All right, put him here. Put him here ...

Reg (*lowering Norman on to the terrace steps*) Right. Down you come ...

Norman Thank you very much. Much obliged.

Reg Bit of fresh air should sober him up.

Sarah I have never known anyone who can ruin an evening as thoroughly as he can.

Norman Nobody loves me.

Sarah Norman . . .
Norman Nobody loves me at all.
Reg Shouldn't think so.
Sarah Norman! Norman, listen to me—will you stop feeling sorry for yourself. Anything that's happened to you is entirely your own fault.
Reg It's the fault of that home-made wine, if you ask me.
Sarah Reg . . .
Reg What?
Sarah Would you mind leaving us for a moment and doing something useful.
Reg What?
Sarah I don't know. Go and talk to Tom.
Reg Tom's gone home.
Sarah Well, you could wash up the supper things. That wouldn't hurt you for once.
Reg Annie's doing that, isn't she? She doesn't want me.
Sarah Annie is seeing to Mother. Anyway, we're supposed to be down here in order to give Annie a rest.
Reg We're supposed to have come down here in order that she can go away.
Sarah Well, she obviously isn't going away, is she? Not with this one.
Reg I don't know why you didn't let them instead of interfering.
Sarah Do you honestly believe it was me that stopped them going? Do you think I could have stopped them for a minute if they'd really wanted to go? If Annie had really wanted to go?
Reg I think you'd have had a good try. All right, I'll do the washing up.
Sarah And put an apron on first otherwise you'll ruin those trousers.
Reg You know, I wouldn't have missed this week-end for anything in the world . . .

Sarah fetches a cushion from the window-seat and sits by Norman

Reg goes in

Sarah Norman . . .
Norman Sarah, we're alone at last.
Sarah Norman.
Norman Mmm?
Sarah I think it's about time we had a talk.
Norman Oh, no—don't bother, honestly, Sarah. (*He puts his head in Sarah's lap*) I'll just curl up here in the garden. I won't be any more trouble, I promise you.
Sarah Norman.
Norman What?
Sarah Are you listening to me?
Norman Yes, yes . . .
Sarah I've no wish to waste my time with you if you're not going to listen to me. I've a dozen things I could be doing at home. I've got two children to worry about, a house, a husband—of sorts.

Norman puts his hand on Sarah's knee. Sarah gets up. Norman's head falls
on the cushion. Sarah looks in the house, fetches a second cushion from the
window-seat, closes the door, and sits by Norman

But the point is I seem to be the only one in this family capable of making any decision at all.

Norman lies straight, his head on the cushion

I mean, whether I like it or not, I seem to be the head of this family at the moment. By rights, it ought to be Reg—if you've lived with Reg, you know he can't even pay a gas bill. How he's still an estate agent after all these years I never cease to wonder. I'm amazed he hasn't sold someone the same house twice . . .

Norman What's wrong with that? That's standard estate agent's practice, isn't it?

Sarah Did you stop for a minute and seriously think of what you were doing when you asked Annie away this week-end? Did you ever think what the consequences might be?

Norman Ruth wouldn't care. She doesn't care.

Sarah I'm not worried about you and Ruth, your—well, what you do is your business—I'm thinking of Annie. What about her?

Norman She'd have had a good week-end. I'd have given her that. What have you ever given her? What's anyone ever given her?

Sarah Very noble of you . . .

Norman Not noble. She'd have probably given me a good week-end.

Sarah And what would have happened to her and Tom?

Norman He'd never have known.

Sarah He'd have found out.

Norman Meaning you would have told him?

Sarah No. Annie would have done.

Norman Annie? She's not that stupid . . .

Sarah She's in love with him.

Norman With Tom?

Sarah Yes.

Norman Rubbish. You've seen them together. She kicks him round the place like an old football. A punctured football. He doesn't even bounce back.

Sarah If she kicks him, it's probably the only way she can get any reaction from him at all. What else is a woman supposed to do if she's stuck with a man like that.

Norman Tom doesn't love anybody. Except cats and bull terriers—she's damn lucky he's so even tempered. I told him—the way she treats him —he ought to take a swing at her.

Sarah I'm sure she'd prefer that to being ignored.

Norman She doesn't want Tom . . . Stop trying to push everybody together, that cat's still up there. (*Calling*) Puss, puss, puss. He's gone now. You can come down . . . (*To Sarah*) Present company excepted, the trouble with the men in this house—and I include your husband—

is they allow themselves to be trampled on by the giant feet of their
cow elephant spouses.

Sarah Whose fault's that?

Norman Just because Reg happens to be a very gentle friendly soul—just
because Tom happens to be a man who's never had an aggressive
thought in his little head, in his little life, doesn't mean it's a cue for
every woman in sight to bounce up and down on them like nubile lady
trampoline artists—what have you done to him? Look at him, in there,
little Reg in his pinny, busy with his little bridget brush polishing away.
Polishing the plates for dear life because Sarah said so.

Sarah While you're lying out here stinking of drink.

Norman That's a man's role. To lie about stinking of drink.

Sarah I bet you've never washed up in your life.

Norman I line up the dishes and smash them—slowly—with the steak
tenderizer—remind me, I'll give Reg one for Christmas. That'd give
you something to complain about.

Sarah You really don't understand me at all, do you? You don't like me
and you've never tried to understand me . . .

Norman I understand you.

Sarah But you don't like me? Do you?

Norman I—don't dislike you. You make me irritable. You're like—mild
athlete's foot.

Sarah I see.

Norman I'll tell you. When I was at my primary school—mixed infants—
we had a little girl just like you. She was very pretty, very smart and clean
—beautifully dressed—always a nicely starched little frock on—nicely
ironed bow in her hair—butter wouldn't melt anywhere. Let alone her
mouth. And she ran that little school with more sheer ruthless efficiency
than the head of the Mafia. She asked you to do something for her and
you did it. You never argued. It was no good arguing with her. She was
cleverer than you were. Precociously clever. She could reduce a nine-
year-old thug to tears with her sarcasm. And it was no use trying to
thump her, either. She'd seduced all the best muscle in the place. She
had a body-guard five deep. Not that she ever needed it. For some reason,
she took a real dislike to me. Maybe because she could see what I really
thought of her. She made my life murder. I was terrified to go to school.
I used to pretend to be sick—I used to hide—play truant—anything rather
than go. And then one day, in the holidays, she came round with her
mother to our house to see my mother. A sociable tea and chat. And
they sent us two out on our own to play together. And suddenly there we
were, not in the school, not in the playground—which was definitely her
territory—but on mine. My garden, my patch. And we stood there and
we just looked at each other. And I thought what am I frightened of you
for? A skinny little girl with knock knees and a front tooth missing—
what on earth have I been frightened of you for, for heaven's sake?
(*Standing*) So I picked her up, like this under one arm and I carried her
right down the bottom of the garden by the rubbish tip—she never
made a sound during this, not a word, nothing—and I found the biggest

patch of stinging nettles I could find and I pulled down her knickers and sat her right in the middle of them. I felt marvellous. It was a beautiful moment. Magic. And she sat there for a very long time—not moving, just looking at me—weighing me up, you know. Then she got up, pulled up her knickers, very quietly took hold of my hand, gave me a big kiss and we went in and had our tea. I've never been in love like that again. (*He sits close to Sarah*)

Sarah I don't believe a word of that.

Norman It may have been an allegory.

Sarah Really? Meaning what?

Norman Meaning, watch it. This garden's full of nettles.

Sarah I believe you would, too. If you weren't so drunk.

Norman I would if I thought you'd give me a kiss . . . (*He reaches out and touches her hand*)

Sarah (*without moving her hand away*) Oh, Norman. Ruth, then Annie, then me. Be your age.

Norman (*taking her hand more firmly*) I don't mean any harm . . .

Sarah You're so dopey, I don't know how anybody could fall for you.

Norman God knows. (*He kisses her hand*) Animal magnetism.

Sarah You've no morals. No nothing, have you?

Norman I'm full of love.

Sarah And wine . . .

Norman (*moving closer*) By God, you're lovely.

Sarah (*snatching away her arm*) Now, Norman. That's enough . . .

Norman (*kneeling up by her*) Going to call Reg, are you?

Sarah (*remaining where she is*) That's enough . . .

Norman kisses her swiftly

Enough . . .

Norman (*softly*) Help, help, Reg . . .

Sarah That's enough, I said. (*She kisses him*) Quite enough—(*She kisses him*) No more . . .

Norman Sorry.

Sarah Enough. (*She kisses him again. This time it develops into a long kiss. Passionately*) Oh, my God, what am I doing . . .

Norman (*kissing her all over*) I know what you're doing. Don't worry. I'll tell you later.

Sarah (*struggling free*) Norman—Norman—I'll get you something to eat, Norman.

Norman (*persisting*) I've got you—that's enough . . .

Sarah (*still struggling*) No—please—Norman—please—let me get you something to eat—and then I'll come back . . . Norman. (*She pulls away finally and rises*)

Norman Where are you going, Sarah?

Sarah (*breathless*) I want to get you something to eat. I want you to eat something—please let me get you something to eat. I'll come back.

Norman Come back.

Sarah As soon as I've got you something . . .

Annie comes out of the house

A silence

Annie Oh, I'm sorry. Were you having a private conversation?

Sarah (*in some disarray*) No—no. I was just getting Norman something to eat . . .

Sarah goes inside

Annie What's the matter with her?

Norman How do you mean?

Annie Well, she's all—jittery.

Norman No.

Annie Have you two been getting at each other again?

Norman Well—here and there.

Annie You've never got on with her, have you? I know she's difficult. I mean, she drives me up the wall sometimes . . . but honestly, Norman, if you can just try and be nice to her—it does pay off.

Norman I'll bear it in mind. (*He lies flat*)

Annie Look at you, you old tip . . . (*She kicks him*)

Norman Don't do that.

Annie Lovely night. I had to read to Mother. She wouldn't go off to sleep for ages. I wouldn't mind but she likes these awful books.

Norman What sort? Horror stories, knowing her.

Annie They wouldn't be so bad. I don't object to horror stories. No, she insists on all these torrid romances. I mean, really. It's bad enough having to buy them, with their incredible front covers—I have to wrap them round with copies of *Country Life* to carry them home. But then having to read them out loud—it's awfully embarrassing. And you can't skip anything. Come on, she says, come on they did more than that, come on.

Norman She's an evil lady, that one. No wonder you're all peculiar.

Annie Norman.

Norman Uh?

Annie Look, I know why you got drunk tonight? (*She sits beside him*)

Norman Oh. You've guessed my secret.

Annie It was because I let you down, wasn't it?

Norman Good Lord, no.

Annie I feel really dreadful.

Norman Think nothing of it.

Annie The worst thing is, we planned the week-end in January—we talked and wrote about it for six months—and you go ahead and get it all organized and—well, I don't think I really could have gone, anyway. It was just a dream. Something you think about but never really mean to do. And then you turn up here and . . .

Norman The dream's shattered.

Annie What I'm saying is, don't blame Sarah. She merely said what I was feeling. You mustn't take it out on her. You mustn't hate her.

Norman Right.

Annie It's my fault. I'm a coward.

Norman Forget it.

Annie Tom was awfully odd this evening. I don't think he knows, but I think he suspects. He was almost rude for Tom. Told me I looked like an old post office sack or something.

Norman Good God, the man's a sadist.

Annie I suppose I do a bit. I think I'm going to make one of my efforts tomorrow. I haven't made an effort for a bit.

Norman You're fine.

Annie Norman, look. I'm going to say something. But you're not to look at me while I'm saying it—do your promise?

Norman What do you intend to do while you're saying it, may I ask?

Annie Nothing. It's just I'll get embarrassed if you do . . .

Norman You're going to read me one of Mother's books, aren't you?

Annie Oh, Norman. This is frightfully difficult. Please . . .

Norman Sorry. Won't look.

Annie I promised you this week-end. I promised I'd go away with you and that I'd stay with you in a hotel and—everything. Well, I've let you down. I've been a coward.

Norman No, no . . .

Annie I think the bit that made me a coward was the going away bit, really. The actual thing of going into a hotel. All that pretending. It just isn't really me. I'd just get embarrassing and stupid.

Norman Never.

Annie Anyway. I'm not a coward about anything else . . . do you get what I mean?

Norman No.

Annie Oh, for heaven's sake . . . if you want to come to my room tonight, you'll be very welcome, that's all. You can look now.

Norman looks. A pause

Well?

Norman Well.

Annie I suppose I've done that all wrong, too.

Norman Not at all. Not at all.

A pause

Annie Well. Say something. Even if it's only thank you.

Norman Er—what time?

Annie What?

Norman Would you like me to come? What time would you like me to come?

Annie Well—when you like—I don't know. Don't make it too late, I'll be asleep.

Norman Right. It's just I've got one or two things to do first . . .

Annie Suit yourself. I'm going up to make up your bed. Just for appearances, I should get into it and make it look used. You know . . .

Norman Good point, yes.
Annie Just for Sarah's benefit.
Norman What?
Annie In case she . . .
Norman Yes, right. I'll mess it up for Sarah.
Annie Well . . .
Norman Well . . .
Annie See you later then?
Norman Right.

Annie kisses Norman

Reg appears in an apron holding a salad basket

Reg (*seeing them*) Oh. Beg your pardon, beg your pardon . . .
Annie What for?
Reg (*winking*) Sorry, sorry. I saw nothing. Nothing at all. Don't worry.
   (*Holding up the salad basket*) Sarah says, where does this go?
Annie I don't know. Just sling it on top of the cupboard. That's what I
   do.
Reg Oh, right . . .
Annie (*taking it from him*) It's all right. I'll do it, I'm going in. Anyway,
   you've got to know how to sling it . . .

Annie goes indoors

Reg Hallo there, Norman.
Norman Hallo there, Reg. You come to seduce me?
Reg Eh?
Norman Nothing.
Reg Ah. That's done that, anyway. I hate washing up. Look at these
   hands. Ruined. (*He laughs*) Hey, I'm going to get myself a drink. Do
   you want one?
Norman Great.
Reg Think we've earned one.
Norman Bring the bottle.
Reg Right.

Reg goes in

Norman This boy can do no wrong tonight. He has the Midas touch.
   Every woman turns to gold. (*Shouting at the cat*) Come down here, cat.
   You don't know what you're missing.

Reg reappears with a bottle and two glasses

Reg Who are you shouting at?

Norman points

Oh, yes. Hallo, pussy. Here we are. The last of mother's home-made parsnip.

Norman takes the bottle from him. Reg holds out two glasses. Norman fills one and wanders away with the bottle

Don't you want a glass?

Norman I'll drink from the bottle. I'm all man tonight.

Reg (*sitting on the barrel*) Wish I was. I'm clapped out. Cheers. (*He drinks*)

Norman Good health, Reg. (*He swigs*) Ah, it's a good night, Reg. It's a lovely night.

Reg Beautiful . . .

Norman It's on a night such as this that all the old base instincts of primitive man, the hunter, come flooding up. You long to be away—free—filled with the urge to rape and pillage and conquer.

Reg I've just got the urge to put my feet up. I think my ankles are swelling again. (*He rolls up his trouser-legs and takes off his shoes and one sock*)

Norman My God! I'm filled with the lust for conquest tonight.

Reg (*examining his legs*) I'm going to get varicose veins if I'm not careful. That'll be the next thing. I've just about got everything else . . .

Norman (*excitedly*) Reg, I have this tremendous idea. I want to tell you about this tremendous idea, Reg. May I tell you about my tremendous idea?

Reg All right, yes, if you want to . . .

Norman It's suddenly come to me, this tremendous idea. It's terrific. Let's all of us—you, me, Tom—let's take a couple of weeks and just go . . .

Reg Go? Where?

Norman Anywhere. Just we men . . .

Reg Do you mean a holiday?

Norman Well, in a way—no, not a holiday—that sounds so damn conventional. I want us just to go. And see things. And taste things. And smell things. And touch things—touch trees—and grass—and—and earth. Let's touch earth together, Reg.

Reg Where were you thinking of going?

Norman Everywhere. Let's see everywhere. Let's be able to say—we have seen and experienced everything.

Reg We'd have to be going some to do that in two weeks, wouldn't we?

Norman I've never really looked before, you know, Reg. These kids today, you know, they've got the right ideas. This world is my world and I'm going to wrap my arms right round it and hug it to me.

Reg I'd go easy on that stuff, you know . . .

Norman In one great big bloody beautiful embrace.

Reg Yes. Ssh, now quietly, Norman. Mother's asleep.

Norman When you think of the things we've done with our lives—our little lives up to this moment—you realize—what a waste. What a dreadful waste. (*To the heavens*) Please don't let me die till I've seen it. Please don't let me die.

Reg (*rising anxiously*) It's all right, Norman. You're not going to die, it's
all right.
Norman (*turning and embracing Reg*) Oh, Reg . . .
Reg Ssh. Steady on. Steady on. Quietly . . .
Norman (*tearfully*) You're my brother, Reg, my brother.
Reg Yes, well, brother-in-law, yes. (*He tries to disentangle himself*) Look,
Norman . . .
Norman Let's stop hating and start to love, Reg.
Reg Ssh. Yes, yes—good idea . . .
Norman I love you, Reg. I'm not ashamed to say that to my brother. I
love you.
Reg That's good news, Norman, yes.

> *Sarah enters with a plate of sandwiches. She stops as she sees the men
> Annie, alarmed by the noise, enters separately behind her, pillow-case in
> hand*

Norman I love you, Reg, I love you.

> *Norman collapses clasping Reg's knees. Reg looks at the women. Annie and
> Sarah look at each other, then back at Reg*

Reg He's—er—he's obviously had a—he's had a—he's . . . (*He pauses*)
Sarah We'd better get him inside.
Reg Yes.

> *Sarah puts down her plate. They gather round Norman preparing to drag
> him inside. Norman starts sobbing*

He's crying.
Sarah He's drunk. That's all he is, drunk. Come on, we'll have to pull
him. I'm not lifting him. Come on—pull . . .

> *Reg starts to haul Norman into the house*

Norman (*as he goes; tearfully, to Sarah*) Nobody loves me. (*To Annie*)
Nobody loves me . . .

> *Reg hauls Norman into the house. Sarah picks up Reg's shoes and follows.
> Annie picks up the sandwiches and cushions and goes in after Sarah: she
> looks out of the window, then disappears*

CURTAIN

ACT II

SCENE 1

The same. Sunday, 11 a.m.

Ruth is standing thoughtfully. Sarah is moving around with an insecticide spray, spraying the roses. Two slightly ancient collapsible garden chairs are leaning against the barrel

Ruth Well.

Sarah Yes.

Ruth Norman and Annie. Well, well.

Sarah Yes. I thought you ought to know.

Ruth Thank you for phoning me. I don't know what I'm expected to do, though.

Sarah Well . . .

Ruth I mean, one can't take it very seriously. It's obviously only another of Norman's gestures against the world or whatever. It's not as if they've even done anything.

Sarah I think you might've done a little more than just laugh. I mean, if I'd been in your position I certainly would have . . .

Ruth Sarah, dear, I've been married to Norman for five years. I have learnt through bitter experience that the last thing to do with Norman is to take him seriously. That's exactly what he wants. I'm not saying it isn't a strain sometimes to keep smiling when he's behaving particularly bizarrely and threatening to burn down the house. When he really gets on top of me, I just go to bed and lock the door.

Sarah I'm amazed you've stayed with him, I really am.

Ruth Well, I don't really look at it that way. I rather think of him as staying with me. After all, I make all the payments on the house, most of the furniture is mine. It has crossed my mind, in moments of extreme provocation, to throw him out—but I don't know, I think I must be rather fond of him. It's a bit like owning an oversized unmanageable dog, being married to Norman. He's not very well house-trained, he needs continual exercising—mental and physical—and it's sensible to lock him up if you have visitors. Otherwise he mauls them. But I'd hate to get rid of him.

Sarah That's all very well if you keep him under proper control. When he goes upsetting other people's lives. Annie's, for example . . .

Ruth You really can't blame Norman entirely, you know. He only jumps up at people who encourage him. It's a general rule, if you don't want him licking your face, don't offer him little titbits. I don't mean just Annie either.

Sarah I don't know what you're talking about.

Ruth Oh, come on, Sarah, I'm sure at some time he's cast an eye in your direction.

Sarah Certainly not.

Ruth In fact I've seen him do it.

Sarah Rubbish. Don't assume everyone's motives are the same as your own. Anyway, the point is, so far as I can gather, Annie and Tom are practically not on speaking terms. They had words, apparently, last night. I don't think he knows about Norman, but all the same, Tom senses something. He's very upset.

Ruth Oh, she's not still with that limp man . . .

Sarah Tom would make her a very good husband. I mean, he may have his faults but when you compare him to some men—he's kind, very considerate. He's done a lot for Annie over the years . . .

Ruth He's as selfish as hell.

Sarah That is just not true . . .

Ruth He is quite content, from all accounts, to come round here day after day, eat her food, use the place as a second home—come and go just as he pleases and what's he given her in return? Absolutely nothing.

Sarah I think that's extremely unfair.

Ruth He's a parasite. Like one of the tics on his wretched animals.

Sarah Oh well, it's obviously not worth discussing this with you. We don't see eye to eye on anything. We never have.

Ruth (*taking one of the chairs and starting to put it up*) Quite right. Very sensible. I'm going to enjoy a bit of sun. Then I'm going home to do some work. It was very kind of you to phone me and express so much concern over my relationship with Norman. As I say, there's nothing I can do about it, Norman is a law unto himself and always has been and I have a mountain of work to do by tomorrow—what the hell's wrong with this chair? (*She struggles to put it up*)

Sarah If you'd wear your glasses it would help.

Ruth Oh, don't you start on me about my glasses. Norman's bad enough.

Sarah You grope about—drive cars . . .

Ruth Look, go away, Sarah. You're a pain in the neck.

Sarah I think Norman's just about what you deserve, I really do . . .

Ruth (*still grappling*) Damn and blast this thing . . .

Sarah Here, come on, let me . . .

Ruth (*fiercely*) Oh, go away.

Sarah All right, all right. I still don't know why you won't wear your glasses. They're a great improvement.

Sarah goes into the house

Ruth glares after her. She has one final go at the chair, then finally perches on it uncomfortably, upright, still unopened

Tom wanders on by the statue

Tom Oh. Ruth. Hallo.

Ruth Who's that?

Tom goes near enough for her to see who it is

Oh—hallo.

Tom You're here?

Ruth Yes.

Tom Ah.

Tom notices the way Ruth is sitting on her chair. He studies her for a moment, puzzled

Er . . .

Ruth What?

Tom Nothing. I—er . . . (*Gesturing vaguely towards her chair*) Nothing.

Tom selects the other chair, is about to put it up then decides, perhaps out of courtesy, to sit on it the same as Ruth is doing on hers

Seen Norman?

Ruth Yes.

Tom Ah. Seen Annie?

Ruth Yes.

Tom Ah.

A pause

Ruth I've also seen Reg and Sarah—in fact, I think I've seen just about everybody there is to see.

Tom Ah. Now you've seen me.

Ruth Yes. I've seen you.

Tom You look—different. Can't think why. Different.

Ruth I'm older, perhaps.

Tom No, no—can't think. It'll come to me. (*A pause*) Er . . .

Ruth What?

Tom I was just wondering if there was any reason why we were sitting like this.

Ruth I don't know why you should be.

Tom No, nor do I.

Ruth I know why I am.

Tom Oh? Why?

Ruth Because I can't put the bloody thing up.

Tom (*leaping into action*) Oh. Well. Just a sec. Excuse me. Hang on. (*He puts the chair up*) Here we are.

Ruth Thank you.

They both sit, Tom on his chair still unopened

Tom You've seen Annie, you say?

Ruth Yes.

Tom Ah. How did she look?

Ruth Aren't you going to put your chair up?

Tom Oh, yes. Good idea.

Tom puts up his chair and sits

Ruth Annie looks very well. From what I've seen.
Tom The point is—I think I'm in her bad books.
Ruth Really?
Tom Yes. I rather went at her last night. Tore her off a strip.
Ruth You did?
Tom Yes, I thought it might—well, she seemed to be taking me far too much for granted.
Ruth Was she?
Tom So I thought a couple of sharp words might do the trick. I told her to straighten herself up.
Ruth Did you?
Tom Told her she looked a mess.
Ruth Really.
Tom Yes. I threatened to belt her. Really let rip.
Ruth I see.
Tom I haven't slept a wink. Do you think I've damaged my chances?
Ruth Chances of what?
Tom I don't know. Just general chances.
Ruth Well. Some women do respond awfully well to that sort of treatment. They enjoy tremendously being told they look a mess—and they actually thrill to the threat of physical violence. I've never met one that does, mind you, but they probably do exist. In books. By men. But then, there are probably some women who enjoy being thrown into canals. One just doesn't bump into them every day—not even in this family.
Tom You reckon I might possibly have been on the wrong track?
Ruth I'd have thought so.
Tom Oh, well. For once he was wrong.
Ruth Who was wrong?
Tom Norman.
Ruth Norman? Did Norman tell you to do that?
Tom He suggested I do something of the sort.
Ruth Insult her and threaten to beat her up?
Tom Yes. He's generally right. About women, anyway. He's got a good instinct, has Norman. Has a way with women. I shouldn't really be saying this, should I?
Ruth (*after looking at Tom for a while incredulously*) Tom.
Tom Um?
Ruth At the risk of pouring bad advice on bad, I think perhaps I ought to point you in the right direction.
Tom Do. Yes, do. Any advice . . .
Ruth Firstly, there are fallacies in Norman's well-known universal theory of womanhood with which, as it happens as his wife, I am familiar. He claims that women can be divided into two groups—the ones you stroke and the ones you swipe. There has been some research done on this and it's been discovered quite recently that they are actually a little more complex.

Tom Yes, yes. It follows . . .

Ruth Good. They enjoy flattery no less than a man does. Though if you are flattering a woman, it pays to be a little more subtle. You don't have to bother with men, they believe any compliment automatically . . .

Tom Oh, come on. Hardly, hardly . . .

Ruth Well, we won't argue that. All I'm saying is, Tom, you're an intelligent man, you're not unattractive . . .

Tom Oh well, thank you very much.

Ruth And you obviously feel a lot of things that you don't show—necessarily. Which is marvellous in a crisis but a bit disheartening in times of peace.

Tom How do you mean?

Ruth I think you have to give a little. Give, Tom, do you see?

Tom Ah.

Ruth Do you follow me?

Tom (*comprehending*) Aha—yes. (*He sits back and ponders this*) Give a little what?

Ruth Oh, my God. (*Impatiently*) You're a very frustrating person to talk to, Tom. I feel like a tame mouse on one of those wheels they have in cages—one keeps running round and round like mad getting nowhere.

Tom That's interesting you should mention that. There have been some studies done. Mice and wheels and it's really quite remarkable. One of the things they discovered . . .

Ruth Yes, right. Thank you.

Tom Eh?

Ruth Don't let's wander off the subject.

Tom No.

Ruth (*studying him*) I think your brain works all right. I think what must happen is, it receives a message from the outside—but once that message gets inside your head, it must be like an unfiled internal memo in some vast Civil Service department. It gets shunted from desk to desk with nobody willing to take responsibility for it. Let's try some simple reactions, shall we? I hate you, Tom. Do you hear? I hate you.

Tom Um?

Ruth Oh well, try again. I love you, Tom. I love you.

Tom (*laughing nervously*) I don't quite get this—a game, is it?

Ruth No, Tom, it is not a game. It's an attempt to communicate.

Tom Ah.

Ruth You're refreshing after Norman, I'll give you that. Who is never one to hide anything. He has three emotions for every occasion.

Tom I know what it is. Why you look different. You're not wearing your glasses.

Ruth No.

Tom Makes a great difference to you, that. Without your glasses.

Ruth Thank you, Tom. That's good. You're learning.

Tom I think I prefer you with them on, actually. It gives your face a better shape. (*Gesturing vaguely*) Sort of . . .

Ruth (*menacing*) Tom . . .

Tom Um?

Ruth Do you get on well with your animals, by any chance?

Tom Yes, yes, generally . . .

Ruth You amaze me. You have a disastrous effect on me, did you know that?

Tom Oh.

Ruth Everything tends to boil over ever so slightly.

Tom Oh. It's pretty warm.

Ruth I have a desire to put on my glasses and take off my clothes and dance naked on the grass for you, Tom. I'd put on my glasses not in order to improve the shape of my face, but in order to see your reaction, if any. And as I whirled faster and faster—the sun glinting on my lenses —flashing messages of passion and desire, I would hurl you to the ground, rip off your clothes and we would roll over and over making mad, torrid, steaming love together. How does that grab you, Tom?

Tom (*after a moment*) Good Lord. (*He laughs*) Have to be careful where you rolled on this grass.

Ruth Oh. (*She sits back exhausted, head in hands*)

Tom (*watching her anxiously*) Ruth? Are you all right? Fairly hot this sun. Nearly overhead. (*Rising*) Perhaps you ought to have a lie down . . .

Ruth I'm sorry. I'm exhausted. I've done my best. I'm sorry.

Tom (*flapping round her*) Can I get you an aspirin?

Ruth lies back with her eyes closed. Tom moves anxiously back to his chair and sits

Look, I had no idea you felt like this. I honestly had no idea.

Ruth Like what?

Tom Like that. With me.

Ruth (*through gritted teeth*) I have never hidden my feelings towards you, Tom.

Tom I had no idea . . .

Ruth What are you talking about, Tom?

Tom I feel terrible about this. Absolutely terrible. This has complicated things no end. I mean, it looks as if the ball's in my court rather. Yes, you've bowled me a googly there.

Ruth What the hell is a googly?

Tom If a woman, unexpectedly, suddenly tells you she loves you, where do you go from there?

Ruth Are we talking theoretically?

Tom If you like.

Ruth Well, it's rather up to you then, isn't it? Firstly, you have to ask yourself, do I love her.

Tom Well, I haven't had much time to think. I mean, love's a bit strong. Anyway, there's somebody else.

Ruth What are you talking about?

Tom Well, there's Norman. I've got to think of Norman's feelings.

Ruth Norman? Don't be so damned ridiculous. As far as Norman's concerned, this is some passing romantic pipe-dream. So stop using Norman as an excuse for your own inadequacy. If you don't grab quickly, somebody else will sooner or later. Someone with a little more determination than Norman ever had.

Tom Well, I'm sorry. That's all I can say. I had no idea. Does Norman know, do you think?

Ruth What?

Tom About me?

Ruth Of course he knows.

Tom Oh, that explains it. That's why he's been a bit odd towards me. Slightly strained, you know. (*He rises and wanders, ending up behind his chair*) Oh well. (*A pause*) You're looking very nice, by the way. Lovely. Very nice indeed. Very well turned out.

Ruth I think you're a raving lunatic.

Tom (*modestly*) Well, I go a bit over the moon, sometimes. You don't need to worry.

Annie comes out. She has made her effort. She has done her hair, made up a little and has a dress on

Tom Oh, hallo.

Annie Hallo. You both want some coffee out here?

Tom Oh, well . . .

Ruth (*getting up*) No. I've had enough sun. I think I'll go and brave Mother. (*She goes towards the house, leaving her handbag*)

Annie Yes, she's awake. I've just been in with her.

Ruth Right. (*Passing close to Tom*) Talk to her.

Tom Eh?

Ruth Tell her.

Tom Oh.

Annie You want coffee, Tom?

Tom No, that's all right. (*Studying Annie*) You know, you look different somehow. What is it?

Ruth (*as she goes*) She probably hasn't got her glasses on.

Ruth goes in

Tom No. It isn't that. It'll come to me.

Annie Don't force it.

A pause

Did you catch the cat?

Tom Yes. He was round the front there, when I arrived. Sitting in the sun, purring away.

Annie Good. Is his paw better?

Tom Oh, yes. It wasn't anything serious really—I . . .

Annie The way you went on about it, I thought you were going to have to amputate a leg.

Tom No, well—actually, you may not have noticed but you probably seem to have the unhealthiest cat in the country.

Annie He hasn't had a day without something. He's either got feeble resistance or else he's a terrific hypochondriac. I don't know which. It's the only cat I know with a personal physician.

Tom I'm afraid I do rather use him actually. As a reason for coming.

Annie Well, there's no need. You're welcome any time. It seems a bit unfair to keep pumping him full of medicine, just as an excuse for a meal.

Tom I don't quite do that . . .

Annie Well . . .

Tom Yes.

Annie Any time.

Tom Thanks.

A pause

Annie Tom. I've got to tell you something. (*She sits in one of the chairs*)

Tom Yes. So have I. (*He sits in the other chair*)

Annie Yes, well let me tell you mine first. I think I know what you're going to say and this may make all the difference. The point is that this week-end Norman asked me to go away with him.

Tom Norman?

Annie Yes. He wanted us to go away together for a week-end. As you see we didn't go, but—I thought you ought to know that we were considering it. I nearly agreed. There, I've said it. That's it.

Tom (*slowly*) I see.

Annie I'm sorry.

Tom No—no . . .

Annie Are you hurt?

Tom Well—I understand—I think . . .

Annie You do? You wouldn't have wanted me to go, would you?

Tom No. But I don't think I'd have had the right to stop you.

Annie Yes, well, maybe not—technically. I know we're not that close. All the same, I thought you might have felt . . .

Tom No, it's not that. It's not you. It's just that I think I understand what Norman was doing.

Annie He was asking me away to a hotel.

Tom Yes, I know that. But why was he?

Annie Why does any man?

Tom Yes, yes, yes. But you see, behind all that, in some obscure way, I think he wanted to get back at me.

Annie Get back at you?

Tom He knows, you see.

Annie Knows what?

Tom About Ruth and me.

Annie Ruth and you?

Tom Yes. That's what I wanted to tell you.

Annie You and Ruth?

Tom Yes.

Annie But you haven't—with Ruth . . . ?

Tom No. Not *with* Ruth, no.

Annie Well, with who, then?

Tom No, it is with Ruth but not me with Ruth, rather Ruth with me. There's a difference.

Annie Is there?

Tom Yes. You see, it appears that Ruth—you'll have to bear with me, this is fraught with embarrassment—Ruth, you see—I'm so useless at this, I never pick up these signals and signs and hints till it's far too late. Ruth's apparently been carrying a torch for me.

Annie She has?

Tom I didn't encourage her, I promise you. As a matter of fact, I didn't even know. 'Till just now.

Annie Are you sure you've got this right, Tom? Ruth can be a little— well, quick, you know. I mean, I'm not saying you did, but could you have missed the point?

Tom No. I assure you, I did not miss the point. No chance of that. Rather wish I had. She made it all graphically clear. She wanted to take off her clothes—oh, well it's very embarrassing. I won't go into it.

Annie No, go on. Take off her clothes?

Tom Oh, well she went on, you know. I hate you, I love you—I want to roll about naked in my glasses . . .

Annie Are you sure you got this right?

Tom Yes. She said she'd never belonged to Norman. It was just a pipe-dream—that Norman knew all about it and I'd better grab her while she's still boiling over.

Annie I don't believe it. What did you say?

Tom I was a bit taken aback. I said I'd have to think it over.

Annie (*indignant*) Think it over?

Tom Obviously.

Annie What about me?

Tom Yes, well, that too . . .

Annie Yes, that too . . .

Tom Oh, goodness, this is getting awfully difficult.

Annie Not at all. It's not difficult. Don't let me stand in your way. You rush off.

Tom No—no . . .

Annie Go on. Go on. Good riddance.

Tom No, Annie, I . . .

Annie And in future I'd be grateful if you'd stop molesting our damn cat.

Reg appears in shirt sleeves. He has a tennis ball with him

Reg Right! Here we are. I've got the ball. Catch, Annie . . .

He pretends to throw the ball to Annie

Annie Oh, Reg, not now . . .

Reg Come on. Come on. (*Calling indoors*) Norman! Come on out. We can all do with some exercise. Stuck indoors far too much.

Annie Reg, please, not just at the . . .

Norman comes out. He wears shorts and a tee shirt

Norman Right, where's the action then?
Reg What are you wearing?
Norman Found them upstairs in the cupboard.
Reg I think they're my old ones.
Norman Thank you for the loan. (*Seeing Annie*) Hey-hey! What is this, I see?
Annie What?
Norman Look at her. Just take a look at this beautiful girl.
Reg Oh, yes. She's got a skirt on.
Norman The sunshine has brought the butterfly out of its chrysalis. Isn't she beautiful? (*He pretends to faint*)
Annie All right, Norman, don't overdo it.
Norman No, honestly, you look great. Doesn't she, Tom?
Tom That's what it is. You've got a thing on. A dress. I knew there was something different.
Norman Give the boy a wolf cub badge. (*To Annie*) Fantastic.
Annie Oh, shut up.
Reg Are we going to play a game?
Norman Right.
Annie No.
Norman Oh, come on. Don't get ladylike just because you're in drag.
Reg What are you playing?
Norman I know. I've got it. Strip catch. Every time you drop the ball, you take something off. Here, Annie, catch. (*He mimes throwing the ball to her. Annie reacts*) Missed. Right, get 'em off.
Annie Norman, I'll thump you.
Reg Right. I've got it. Listen. The person with the ball—he calls out somebody's name. And at the same time, he must throw the ball to somebody else. He mustn't throw it to the person whose name he's called out. And he mustn't call his own name. Otherwise, he loses a life. Two lives. And you lose a life if you drop it. Right, here we go. Catch, Tom.

Reg throws the ball to Annie

Tom (*reacting*) What?
Annie (*catching the ball*) Oh. (*She hesitates*)
Reg Keep it going. You must keep it going fast.
Annie Right. Er—Reg.

Annie throws the ball to Norman

Norman Annie.

Norman throws to Tom

Tom Ah. Norman.

Tom throws to Annie

Annie Norman.

Annie throws to Tom

Tom Tom. Oh, no, that's me. Sorry.
Reg Right, that's one life gone.
Tom Sorry—er—Reg.

Tom throws to Annie

Annie Tom.

Annie throws to Norman

Norman Annie.

Norman throws to Reg. Reg drops it

Reg Not too hard. Right, that's one life for me. Annie.

Reg throws to Norman

Norman Annie.

Norman throws to Tom

Tom Annie.

Tom throws to Annie

Oh—sorry . . .
Reg Out! Right, Tom's out.
Tom Sorry. I'm no good at this sort of thing. I'll watch. (*He sits*)
Reg Annie, come on.
Annie Norman.

Annie throws to Reg

Reg Annie.

Reg throws to Norman

Norman Catch it, Reg.

Norman throws to Annie. Annie drops it

Norman (*triumphant*) Ha-ha!

Reg laughs. Annie looks annoyed

Annie Norman.

Annie throws to Reg, who drops it

Reg Steady on, steady on, I wasn't ready.
Norman You were ready, you're out.
Reg No, I wasn't. I wasn't ready. (*To Tom*) You were watching. I wasn't
ready, was I?

Tom Sorry, I missed that.
Norman You're out.
Reg Rubbish
Annie What happens now?
Norman Just us two.
Reg You can't play with just two of you.
Norman Yes, we can.
Reg Don't be daft—I mean . . .
Norman (*throwing the ball to Annie*) Annie.
Annie Norman. (*She throws to him*) This is stupid.
Norman Annie. (*He throws to Annie*) No, it isn't.
Reg Oh well, let 'em play if they want to. (*He sits by Tom*)

*Under the ensuing conversation, Norman and Annie continue their game—
calling each other's name, getting closer together until they are throwing the
ball a few inches distance and finally passing it hand to hand*

Reg How's that car of yours running?
Tom Oh, no complaints. No complaints.
Reg It's funny because my next-door neighbour, he's bought one of those.
  Same year—same model as yours—he's had a lot of bad luck with his.
Tom Has he?
Reg He'd done—what?—eight hundred miles, barely run it in. He's
  starting up this fairly steep hill—in fourth—he changes to third—big
  lorry behind him, big lorry—front of him—finds he needs to change to
  second and whack—whole gear lever comes off in his hand. There he is,
  on this steep hill, stuck in third gear, just about to stall—lorry there—
  lorry there—could have been nasty.
Tom Good Lord.

*Annie and Norman, unseen by them, are now on the ground locked in an
embrace*

Reg As it happens, luckily, he has the presence of mind to turn his wheel
  off the road into the ditch.

*Ruth comes out to collect her handbag which she has left by the chair.
She goes towards Norman and Annie—then peers at them, during the
following*

Safest place. What else could he do? He said, that's the last time I buy
one of those. You won't catch me buying one of those again. You've
been lucky up till now, that's all I can say.
Ruth (*who has been peering at the shape of Norman and Annie on the ground
  for some seconds*) Excuse me, I'm sorry to interrupt, but could you just
  confirm that I'm seeing what I think I'm seeing?

Reg and Tom turn

Reg Flipping heck.
Tom (*rising*) Hey! Hey! (*Moving to Norman and Annie*) Annie—Annie . . .

Annie (*emerging for a second*) Oh, go away.

Ruth Well, throw a bucket of water over them or something.

Tom Annie! (*Angry for him*) All right. Two can play at that. Two can play at that. (*He marches up to Ruth*) I love you, too. Do you hear, I love you, too.

Ruth I beg your pardon.

Tom I love you. (*He grabs Ruth and kisses her*)

Ruth (*struggling furiously*) Tom . . .

Reg stands between the couples, greatly amused

Sarah comes out with a tray

Sarah Now, I'm collecting dirty cups. Are there any . . . Oh, my God. Tom! Tom! Ruth! Norman! Annie! What are you . . . ? Stop them. Somebody stop them. Reg . . .

Reg stands uselessly laughing

Reg, will you do something for once in your life?

CURTAIN

SCENE 2

The same. Monday, 9 a.m.

Ruth enters, ready to leave. She takes one of the chairs and places it level with the barrel. Sarah enters, also dressed ready to go.

Sarah Look at the time. We should be half-way home by now.

Ruth Sorry to hold you up. (*She sits*)

Sarah It gives you a lot of trouble, does it? Your car?

Ruth Now and then. It sometimes starts all right. But only if you're not in a hurry to go anywhere.

Sarah (*fetching the second chair and placing it near Ruth*) Reg'll get it going.

Ruth I hope so.

Sarah It's nice Tom came back this morning. (*She sits*)

Ruth Yes.

Sarah I'm glad he didn't decide to go off in a huff.

Ruth No.

Sarah After yesterday. He could have done.

Ruth He has a forgiving nature.

Sarah Yes. But then I suppose one could say that of you.

Ruth That's one of the hazards of living with Norman. It was much more alarming being attacked by Tom. That I wasn't even expecting.

Reg enters from the tennis court, jacket off, sleeves up, wiping his hands on a rag

Reg Fuse wire. We need a bit of fuse wire.
Sarah Look at your hands.
Reg Well, I've been . . .
Sarah For heaven's sake, don't get it on your shirt.
Reg (*to Ruth*) It's a very dirty engine you've got there. (*He sits on the barrel*)
Ruth Sorry. We seldom get round to washing that.
Reg Let alone the outside.
Ruth It's very kind of you.
Reg No trouble. What I'll do is, I'll bind it on with a bit of fuse wire. It'll only be temporary but it should get you home. She'll still need a shove to start. Could you get it for me?
Sarah What?
Reg Fuse wire.
Sarah Why can't you get it?
Reg Well, look at my hands. I'll get it all over everything.
Sarah Well, I don't see why I . . .
Reg All right, I'll get it myself. I'll only open the door with my teeth.
Sarah (*rising*) Oh, I'll get it then. As usual. What is it you want?
Reg Fuse wire. It's usually in the bottom kitchen drawer. That's where we used to keep it. It's very thin, silver-coloured wire wrapped round a . . .
Sarah I know what fuse wire looks like.
Reg Fine.
Sarah Wait there. I don't know.

Sarah goes into the house

Reg Soon have it fixed.
Ruth Thank you.
Reg I hope so, anyway. We have to get underway soon or she'll be complaining again. I don't know why we're in such a hurry to get home. I don't have to collect the children till this afternoon. Could have enjoyed the sun. You ought to be at work too, oughtn't you?
Ruth I think I've just taken the day off. So has Norman.
Reg Ah well, why not.
Ruth Sarah's being almost amiable towards me at the moment. I don't know why that should be, do you?
Reg No . . .
Ruth I'm afraid I suspect her when she's nice to me. I don't want to sound mean about your wife but whenever she smiles it usually means some disaster is about to overtake me. She was extremely cheerful on my wedding day, I seem to remember.
Reg Ah.
Ruth What's she up to? Do you know?
Reg Well . . .

Ruth What?
Reg (*moving to sit in Sarah's chair*) It's silly but—er—this sounds ridiculous —but do you think Norman has—er . . .
Ruth Has what?
Reg Well—you know. Towards Sarah . . .
Ruth Norman and Sarah?
Reg No, I don't think he can, but—I just has this idea. I think I'm just getting jumpy. He's been round everyone else, hasn't he?
Ruth Everyone else being Annie.
Reg Well, yes. If you like.
Ruth I don't think you should suspect Norman of everything, you know.
Reg No, no—I just . . .
Ruth He can't be held responsible for every strange relationship in this family.
Reg No. I'm sorry. I just . . .
Ruth He's not a complete monster.
Reg No. (*He gets up*)

Sarah enters with a roll of gardening wire

Ah.
Sarah There's none there. Only this. (*She sits in the chair*)
Reg That's garden wire.
Sarah I know it's garden wire. This is all there is.
Reg Worse than useless. Much too thick.
Sarah Well, I'm trying to help.
Reg We need fuse wire. I'll find it, don't worry.
Sarah I've just said there isn't any.
Reg Of course there is. I'll find it.
Sarah You won't you know.
Reg Want a bet?
Sarah Why do you always want to make me out a liar?
Reg You missed it. It's there.
Sarah (*rising*) All right, I'll show you. It isn't there.

Reg and Sarah move towards the house

Reg It's there.
Sarah It is not there.
Reg It's always there.

Reg and Sarah go into the house

Ruth continues to sit

Norman enters from the tennis court

Norman Where's the man with the fuse wire then?
Ruth Arguing with his wife, surprisingly. They can't find it.

Norman Oh.

Ruth Would that have anything to do with you?

Norman Me? I haven't got the fuse wire.

Ruth I mean, them arguing.

Norman (*sitting in the chair*) Glad we're staying at home today.

Ruth I don't think my office will be, particularly

Norman We'll have a great time. Let's do something fun.

Ruth We could wash up.

Norman No.

Ruth There's about two months' worth.

Norman No. That's not fun.

Ruth You could cut our hedge. That man next door complained again. He said he's writing to the council.

Norman Stupid git. Why doesn't he move.

Ruth That's what he said about us.

Norman It's very cruel to cut hedges. Tell him it's against my principles.

Ruth You tell him. So you haven't been making eyes at Sarah?

Norman Sarah?

Ruth In case you'd left anyone out.

Norman Good God. What do you take me for?

Ruth I took you for a husband, Norman. Very foolishly. I can feel my life expectancy shortening minute by minute. After this week-end, it's down by five years.

Norman Don't blame me. I haven't done anything.

Ruth What?

Norman Tom's happy. He's forgiven me.

Ruth Tom is an idiot.

Norman He's a shrewd man. He realized it wasn't serious, Annie and me. Just a mad idea. We were both depressed. I wanted to cheer her up, that's all.

Ruth Well, next time, send her a funny postcard.

Norman There won't be a next time. I'm concentrating on you.

Ruth Oh, God.

Norman I'll be sorry to leave. I like it down here. Must have been nice to grow up in this house. Was it nice?

Ruth All right. I'd nothing against the house. It was the people I didn't care for.

Norman You don't know when you're well off. When I think of my childhood, the little pokey back-to-back terrace . . .

Ruth Overlooking Regent's Park

Norman Hyde Park.

Ruth Well . . .

Norman The unfashionable side. The slums of South Kensington. They were hard days, lass. Anyway, Hyde Park's not country. It's just an underground car park with a grass roof. Shall we have a party tonight?

Ruth No, we won't.

Norman Go on. That'd be fun.

Ruth I'm much too tired.

Norman Right. We'll go to bed. We'll go to bed.

Ruth I said I'm tired.

Norman To rest. We'll rest.

Ruth I know you and your rests. Your mind just doesn't associate beds with sleep at all. I don't know when you do sleep. It certainly isn't with me.

Norman I was brought up to believe it was very insulting to sleep with your wife or any lady. A gentleman stays eagerly awake on one elbow. He sleeps at his work. That's what work's for. Why do you think they have the SILENCE notices in the library? So as not to disturb me in my little nook behind the biography shelves. L–P.

Ruth They'll sack you.

Norman They daren't. I reorganized the Main Index. When I die the secret dies with me. (*He "dies"*)

Tom enters from the tennis court

Tom Well, that's done it.

Norman Done what?

Tom The thing on your car. I've fixed it back on.

Norman I thought we needed wire.

Tom No. It screwed on. Don't need wire.

Norman This vet is a genius.

Tom No. The same thing happened on mine. They're always falling off, those things.

Norman Brilliant.

Ruth Do you think someone should tell Reg? He's still hunting for wire, you know.

Tom Oh, good Lord, is he? I'd better tell him.

Norman No. Let me . . .

Tom It's all right, I'll . . .

Norman Please. Let me. I want to see his face. (*Calling*) Reg . . .

Norman goes off gleefully into the house

Ruth He's so bouncy this morning, I could kick him.

Tom Yes. Well—er . . .

Ruth Oh, do stop looking like that, Tom.

Tom What?

Ruth Embarrassed and furtive.

Tom Well, I was just . . . (*He sits*)

Ruth Forget all about it. It was a misunderstanding.

Tom I don't usually grab hold of women in that way, you know.

Ruth I do realize.

Tom I don't want you to get the impression I . . .

Ruth I haven't.

Tom As long as you appreciate . . . (*He pauses*)

Ruth It's a pity you don't, in a way.

Tom What?

Ruth Grab hold a bit more.

Tom How do you mean?

Ruth Annie, for instance. She might even appreciate it.

Tom Oh, I don't think so. I don't think she goes in for that sort of thing.

Ruth Apart from with Norman.

Tom Ah. (*A pause*) That's a good point. Hadn't looked at it quite like that.

Ruth I think you should.

Tom Women are really dreadfully complicated, aren't they? Or do I mean human beings?

Ruth They can be one and the same.

Tom I mean, with other animals, well the majority of them, they're either off heat or on heat. Everyone knows where they are. I probably should have been born a horse or something. With Annie, I never really know. I mean, just now I was chatting away with her about something or other—she started breaking a plate.

Ruth What?

Tom Smashing a plate. No reason. Just simply smashing a plate. I hardly like to say anything to her, when she's like that. In case she starts on me.

Ruth I think she might, shortly.

Reg comes out angrily. Norman follows, gleeful

Tom rises

Reg (*to Tom*) Well, thank you very much.

Tom All right.

Reg You might have told me it screwed. I've wasted half an hour looking for fuse wire that isn't where it should be.

Tom Sorry. I thought you knew it screwed.

Reg If I'd known it screwed, I wouldn't—and this herbert isn't much help, sniggering away.

Ruth Norman, stop sniggering.

Norman I am not sniggering. These are joyful guffaws.

Reg Did you put the top on again?

Tom No. I thought you might want to . . .

Reg Right. Norman.

Norman What?

Reg Come and do something useful for once.

Norman If it's only for once.

Reg We'll put it together. I'll tow you as far as the top of the hill and then you can roll her down, Ruth. That should start her. Oh. One moment. Have I got my tow rope. I don't think I have. I think I took it out to make room for the cases. Do you carry a tow rope?

Norman No idea. We've lost the key of the boot.

Reg How do you open it?

Ruth We haven't. For months.
Reg Oh, grief . . .

Annie comes out

Norman My gym shoes are in there, too.
Reg Annie.
Norman And my football.
Annie Hallo.
Norman Never mind, it will rust away eventually.
Reg Annie, have we got such a thing as a rope? Big thick one.
Annie I think there's one in the cellar. It's very heavy.
Reg Just the job. Tom.
Tom Um?
Reg You fetch the rope.
Tom Rope?
Annie It's in the cellar. Foot of the steps.
Tom Oh. Right. Rope.

Tom goes into the house

Reg Norman, follow me.

Reg strides off through the tennis court

Norman (*following Reg*) Must be marvellous to be a leader of men.

Norman goes off through the tennis court

Ruth I think we're going to spend another night here at this rate.
Annie Oh well, it's no bother.
Ruth I think it's better if we don't. This country air has a disastrous effect on some of us. Not that I blame anyone particularly. Least of all you. Looking after that woman's enough to turn you completely.
Annie I'm sorry. I've said I'm sorry.
Ruth Why should you be? It was entirely Norman's fault.
Annie Not really. I was feeling lonely and sorry for myself . . .
Ruth Yes, I'm sure you were. That doesn't excuse Norman.
Annie He was lonely, too.
Ruth Norman? Nonsense. What's Norman got to be lonely about? Sorry for himself may be. No, he just can't bear not to be the centre of attention. Anyway, we won't talk about Norman. He gets talked about enough. Which is why he does these things in the first place. You and Tom . . .
Annie Yes.
Ruth Do try and sort out something between you, will you? You can't let it drag on and on. It's really absurd. You both want to get together, you both should. Look, it's a lovely day. As soon as we've all gone, sit Tom down out here and tell him point-blank, either he marries you or

comes and lives with you, or whatever it is you both want, or else he
clears off for good. That'll do it. Be so much more convenient. And then
we wouldn't have to worry about you.

Annie Which would also be convenient.

Ruth Well, we do worry and there's no point in you giving up everything
for Mother's sake. You'll turn into a martyr like Sarah which would be
too dreadful for words. Two of you in the family.

Annie Don't worry.

Ruth You can't sit around smashing crockery for the rest of your life.
It's sometimes quite satisfying but it's no substitute for the real thing.

Annie Who told you about that?

Ruth Tom.

Annie Oh.

Ruth Who else?

Annie No-one.

Sarah comes out, holding some fuse wire

Sarah There. Fuse wire. It wasn't where he said at all. I knew it wasn't.
He wouldn't believe me till he'd seen for himself. Do you know where
I found it?

Annie In the pantry on the second shelf.

Sarah Fancy keeping it in the pantry. Who on earth keeps fuse wire in a
pantry?

Annie People who have fuse boxes in their pantry.

Sarah Look at the time. Where is he then? I'd better give this to him.

Ruth I wouldn't bother.

Sarah Why?

Ruth He doesn't need it.

Sarah Doesn't need it? What do you mean, he doesn't need it?

Reg enters

Reg Now then.

Sarah What do you mean you don't need it?

Reg Need what?

Sarah This fuse wire you've been going on about.

Reg Oh, we fixed that hours ago.

Sarah Do you realize that I have been . . .

Reg We couldn't wait all day for you, could we? Right. We're ready to
go.

Annie What about your rope?

Reg Ah. I had it. Had it all the time. Thought I'd taken it out but I hadn't.

Norman enters

Norman All knots secured, skipper.

Ruth Has he tied the tow rope?

Reg Yes.

Ruth Check it.

Norman What do you mean? We old nautical men. I'll have you know I've crossed the Serpentine in my day. Couldn't do it now, blast it. (*He sits*) Not with this old peg leg.

Ruth Come on, Norman.

Norman gets up

Reg I'll tow you as far as the top of the hill, right? We'll disconnect the rope and then you're free to roll her down. But for heaven's sake wait till I'm out of the way.

Norman This could be fun.

Sarah Come along, we're very late. (*Giving Annie the fuse wire*) Good-bye, Annie. Thank you for—looking after us . . .

Annie You're welcome.

Reg See you at Christmas. If not before.

Sarah I shouldn't think before.

Reg No, no. Well . . .

Ruth 'Bye 'bye, Annie.

Annie 'Bye.

Norman Take care.

Annie Yes.

Sarah 'Bye.

All except Annie start to leave

Reg (*as they go*) Now keep your hand brake on till I give you the word. I don't want you rolling into the back of me.

Ruth All right, all right . . .

They go

Annie watches them out of sight. She turns back to the house

Norman darts on again

Norman (*an urgent whisper*) Annie! Annie!

Annie Norman. What are you . . .

Norman Just came to say good-bye.

Annie Oh, Norman, you're . . .

Norman I'll give you a ring. Can I?

Annie Yes, if you . . .

Norman Next time I'll plan it a bit better, Annie. I promise I'll fix it well in advance—so that . . .

Annie Norman . . .

Norman What?

Annie We can't.

Norman Of course we can. You'd like to, wouldn't you? Wouldn't you?

Annie Yes, but . . .

Norman I'll fix it. Don't worry.

Annie You said that last time. Look what happened. We upset everybody. Ruth, Tom, Sarah.

Norman We love each other, don't we?

Annie (*wearily*) I don't know.

A car horn sounds. Norman dashes behind the statue, then reappears

Norman You'd be happy with me, wouldn't you? You'd be happy.

Annie Yes.

Norman (*moving to embrace her*) Oh, Annie—oh God. (*He is entangled in the brambles*) These damn things again.

Annie All right. Keep still. (*Clearing the brambles*) Keep still.

Norman Oh, Annie—ow!

Annie There we are.

The car horn sounds again

Norman I don't want to lose you, Annie.

Annie They're waiting.

Norman I won't lose you, will I, Annie?

Annie Not if you don't want to . . .

Norman I don't. I really don't.

Two car horns sound in unison

Annie Go on, Norman, go on.

Norman Good-bye, I love you. Good-bye.

Norman goes off through the tennis-court, blowing kisses back to her

Annie Oh, Norman . . . (*She stands for a second*)

Tom comes out from the house laden with a very heavy coil of rope

Tom Here we are. Is this the one? (*Looking round*) Oh. Where are they?

Annie They've gone.

Tom They'll need this.

Annie They've got one.

Tom Oh. Wasted journey.

Annie Yes.

Tom Oh well . . . (*He stands, the rope still on his shoulder, where it remains throughout the scene*) Peace and quiet again, eh?

Annie Yes.

Tom Quite a week-end. (*She sits*)

Annie Yes.

Tom I must say, I'm rather relieved Ruth's gone. After my incident. Bit embarrassing.

Annie Yes.

Tom Expect you're glad to see the back of Norman, aren't you? For the same reason. Yes. You must be. (*Pause*) Look. Annie . . .

Annie Mmm?

Tom (*sitting in the other chair*) I've been piecing things together in my
    mind—fitting the various bits to fill in the picture—building a sort of
    overall view of things—so I can more or less get an objective angle on
    it and—er—well, I expect you know what I'm going to say next?

Annie Honestly, Tom, I couldn't begin to guess.

Tom Oh. Was rather hoping you might. Make it all a bit—save me a—
    it's a shame we're not horses.

Annie What are you talking about, Tom?

Tom Well. It seems to me—that we ought to find a way of—well sorting
    out our relationship—if we have one—to such a degree that we—come
    together more or less on a permanent basis. Temporarily at least.

Annie Are you talking about marriage?

Tom Yes.

Annie Oh.

Tom And no.

Annie Which is it?

Tom Well, it could be a lot looser . . .

Annie As loose as we are now, you mean?

Tom No. I meant a bit tighter than that. Somewhere in between. Well,
    loose and tight. The whole hog if you want to. It's up to you.

Annie I see.

Tom What do you say?

A silence

    Annie . . .

A silence

    Would you like me to marry you? I would. Like me to marry you. May
    I? I want to.

Annie (*at length*) I don't know.

Tom Oh.

Annie I'll see.

Tom Oh. I got the idea that perhaps that's what you would have liked.

Annie I did, I think. I'm sorry, Tom, you'll have to wait.

Tom How long for?

Annie At least until I've had a chance to—go away somewhere. And think
    about it.

Tom Oh, I see. Fair enough.

Pause

Tom Going to be a scorcher today, again.

Annie Yes.

Tom Far too nice to do any work. It's on days like this you really feel
    at peace with the world. That's what I feel . . .

*Two loud horns sound, followed by a distant crash of colliding vehicles.
Annie and Tom jump up*

(*Recovering*) Good grief.

Annie It's them.

Tom Hang on. Stay there. Stay there—this could be nasty.

Annie Quickly, we must . . . (*She starts to move away*)

Tom (*pushing her back*) No, please, Annie—stay there. Stay there.

Tom rushes off through the tennis court

Annie stands anxiously. Loud shouts are heard off

Reg (*off*) You bloody fool.

Reg stamps on followed by Ruth and Sarah. Sarah is flustered. Norman follows up the rear with Tom

Reg What the hell did you let him drive for?

Ruth He insisted.

Tom Everyone all right?

Reg Why him? Why him?

Sarah I feel terribly faint.

Norman You can't expect Ruth to drive.

Reg Why not?

Norman She hasn't got her glasses.

Reg She could drive better than you blindfolded. Where were your brakes?

Tom Any casualties?

Sarah I feel giddy.

Reg I told you distinctly. Wait till I'm out of the way.

Norman My mistake.

Reg Your mistake? You weren't even in gear.

Sarah I need a glass of water.

Tom I'm not a doctor but I am a vet. If anyone needs any treatment.

Annie Is there much damage?

Norman Yes . . .

Ruth hits Norman with his woolly hat, then throws it on the ground. He sits on the barrel.

We smashed his whole back end in.

Reg I know you've smashed the whole back end in. The damn cars are twisted together like bloody spaghetti.

Annie sits Reg down in a chair

Sarah I've never been so shaken.

Ruth Sit down, Sarah.

Sarah sits

Annie Do you want to phone? Phone the AA?

Reg Some people have as much sense as a—you won't get home today, you know that?

Sarah Well, we'll stay, dear, we'll stay.
Reg I'll have to phone home as well. (*Rising*) Somebody get the cases out? I'll do the phoning. (*To Ruth*) Why did you let him drive? You know what he's like? You knew he was Norman, didn't you?

Reg goes indoors

Norman My mistake.
Tom I'll start fetching the cases, shall I?
Sarah Thank you, Tom. I'm so shaky, I . . .
Tom You stay there.
Sarah I will.
Tom Everyone stay there. Reg and I have got it under control.

Tom goes off through the tennis-court. Ruth sits

Norman (*rising*) Definitely my mistake . . . (*He picks up his hat*)

A silence. Norman stands regarding the three women. They look at him

Norman Well. Back again.
Annie Oh, Norman . . . (*She sits on the barrel*)
Ruth If I didn't know you better, I'd say you did all that deliberately.
Norman Me? Why should I want to do that?
Sarah Huh.
Norman Give me one good reason why I'd do a thing like that?
Ruth Offhand, I can think of three.

Pause

Norman Ah. (*Brightening*) Well, since we're all here, we ought to make the most of it, eh? What do you say?

Norman smiles round at the women in turn

Ruth gets up and without another word goes into the house

(*After her*) Ruth . . .

He turns to Annie but she too, rises and goes into the house

Annie . . .

He turns to Sarah. She, likewise, rises and follows the others

Sarah!

Norman is left alone, bewildered, then genuinely hurt and indignant

(*Shouting after them*) I only wanted to make you happy.

CURTAIN

FURNITURE AND PROPERTY LIST

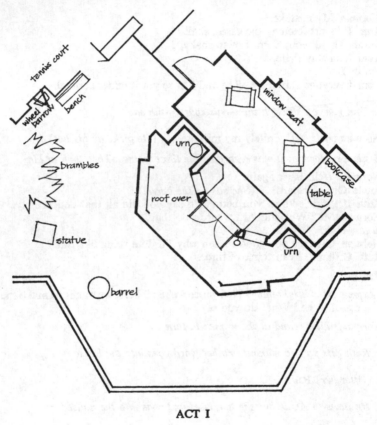

ACT I

SCENE 1

On stage: Garden bench
Wheelbarrow
Half a barrel upturned with empty cup and saucer on it
Statue with brambles over it and trailing
In house:
2 easy chairs
2 cushions on window-seat
Bookcase with lamp on top

Round table with plant

Off stage: Gardening gloves, scissors, 6 roses (Annie)
Small battered suitcase with pair of pyjamas in cellophane (Norman)
2 suitcases (Reg)
Bundle of magazines tied with string (Reg)

Personal: Reg: bag with 1 toffee
Sarah: handbag
Wrist watch for Reg, Sarah, Tom, Annie

SCENE 2

Off stage: Salad basket (Reg)
Apron (Reg)
Bottle of home-made parsnip wine and 2 glasses (Annie)
Pillow-case (Annie)

ACT II

SCENE 1

Set: 2 folding garden chairs leaning against barrel
Ruth's handbag on terrace, down stage end

Off stage: Insecticide spray (Sarah)
Tennis ball (Reg)
Tray (Sarah)

SCENE 2

Off stage: "Grease" for Reg's hands
Rag (Reg)
Roll of gardening wire (Sarah)
Fuse wire (Sarah)
Large coil of rope (Tom)

Personal: Ruth: handbag, watch

LIGHTING PLOT

Property fittings required: exterior lamp, table lamp
Exterior. A garden. The same scene throughout

ACT I, SCENE 1. Evening

To open: Effect of early evening summer sunshine

No cues

ACT I, SCENE 2. Late evening

To open: Patchy light through trees. Exterior lamp on
Table lamp on
No cues

ACT II, SCENE 1. Morning

To open: Effect of bright sunshine

No cues

ACT II, SCENE 2. Morning

To open: As Scene 1

No cues

EFFECTS PLOT

ACT I

SCENE 1

Cue 1   As CURTAIN rises   (Page 1)
            Bird song: continue for a few moments, then fade

SCENE 2

No cues

ACT II

SCENE 1

Cue 2   As CURTAIN rises   (Page 25)
            Bird song as before

SCENE 2

Cue 3   As CURTAIN rises   (Page 37)
            Bird song as before

Cue 4   **Annie:** "I don't know."   (Page 46)
            Car horn

Cue 5   **Annie:** "There we are."   (Page 46)
            Car horn

Cue 6   **Norman:** "I really don't."   (Page 46)
            Two car horns together, impatient

Cue 7   **Tom:** "That's what I feel. . ."   (Page 47)
            2 loud car horns, followed by a crash of colliding vehicles

MADE AND PRINTED IN GREAT BRITAIN BY
LATIMER TREND & COMPANY LTD PLYMOUTH
MADE IN ENGLAND